P9-DLZ-603

FOOLED YA!

FOOLED YA!

HOW YOUR BRAIN GETS TRICKED BY
OPTICAL ILLUSIONS, MAGICIANS, HOAXES & MORE

JORDAN D. BROWN

ILLUSTRATIONS BY
EMILY BORNOFF

CANCELLED

Rocky River Public Library

This book is dedicated to two wonderful people (code names: Avrom and Chaika)
who not only provided the DNA for my easily distracted brain ("What shiny object?"),
but whose boundless generosity, compassion, and humor I try to emulate daily. —J.D.B.

Brimming with creative inspiration, how-to projects, and useful information to enrich your everyday life, Quarto Knows is a favorite destination for those pursuing their interests and passions. Visit our site and dig deeper with our books into your area of interest: Quarto Creates, Quarto Cooks, Quarto Homes, Quarto Lives, Quarto Drives, Quarto Explores, Quarto Gifts, or Quarto Kids.

© 2017 Quarto Publishing Group USA Inc.
Text © 2017 Jordan D. Brown

First Published in 2017 by MoonDance Press, an imprint of The Quarto Group.
6 Orchard Road, Suite 100, Lake Forest, CA 92630, USA.
T (949) 380-7510 F (949) 380-7575 www.QuartoKnows.com

All rights reserved. No part of this book may be reproduced in any form without written permission of the copyright owners. All images in this book have been reproduced with the knowledge and prior consent of the artists concerned, and no responsibility is accepted by producer, publisher, or printer for any infringement of copyright or otherwise, arising from the contents of this publication. Every effort has been made to ensure that credits accurately comply with information supplied. We apologize for any inaccuracies that may have occurred and will resolve inaccurate or missing information in a subsequent reprinting of the book.

MoonDance Press titles are also available at discount for retail, wholesale, promotional, and bulk purchase. For details, contact the Special Sales Manager by email at specialsales@quarto.com or by mail at The Quarto Group, Attn: Special Sales Manager, 401 Second Avenue North, Suite 310, Minneapolis, MN 55401 USA.

ISBN: 978-1-63322-158-1

Illustrations and book design by Emily Bornoff

Printed in China
10 9 8 7 6 5 4 3 2 1

MIX
Paper from responsible sources
FSC® C101537
FSC
www.fsc.org

CONTENTS

Can You Trust Your Brain?

I'M BRIAN D. BRAIN, AND, JUST LIKE YOUR BRAIN, I'M PERFECT ALL THE TIME!

Not always!

Most of us don't give our brains a second thought. But without this squishy blob in your skull, your body would be a messy lump of useless organs and bones. A brainless version of you wouldn't be able to see, hear, smell, taste, or touch. Forget about doing your homework, skiing down a mountain, or inventing an excuse for why you haven't cleaned your room. Without your brain, you've got nothing. Even the automatic functions of your body, such as keeping the heart beating and stomach digesting, rely on your brain. Yes, the brain is an amazing, incredible organ. But it's far from perfect.

That's right, your brain can't always be trusted. It jumps to conclusions, messes up memories, ignores the obvious, and makes dumb decisions. Our brains would like us to think that the world is always an orderly, predictable, and fair place. Ha! Because of the way our brains are wired, many people believe strange things that have no basis in reality, like alien abductions, psychic powers, and unicorns.

I SEE IT NOW. YOU ARE ABOUT TO LOSE A LOT OF MONEY.

FORTUNE TELLER
ONLY $25

On the plus side, our easily fooled brains make it possible for us to enjoy optical illusions and magic tricks. The downside is that our brains make it easier for deceptive people to fool us for non-entertaining reasons. Con artists, pickpockets, advertisers, and pranksters for example, use their knowledge of how the human brain works to take our money or have a laugh at our expense.

Before you get down on your brain for letting you be hoodwinked, bamboozled, and hornswoggled (fancy words for tricked), remember that it is faced with the enormous task of helping you make sense of the world. Every second, the brain is hit with a blizzard of images, sounds, smells, and other sensations all fighting for attention. The brain's job is to sort through all the muck in a flash and help you figure out what to focus on. ("Don't step on that dog poop!" "Grab that last chocolate-chip cookie before your sister swipes it!" "Hey, I'm tired.")

IS THIS GOING TO HURT?

In this book, you'll have many opportunities to experiment with your brain and learn the science behind how the brain sometimes gets stumped.

You'll do a bunch of fun activities that explore each of your senses and discover how they can be fooled in certain situations. You're also going to learn some amazing magic tricks that you can use to dazzle your friends and family. Find out how and why they fool our brains. Along the way, you'll become an expert on the science of how we are tricked by those professional foolers. In fact, after experiencing this book, you'll be a better critical thinker. With this superpower, you'll be able to fight back when others try to "prove" un-scientific ideas, such as astrology and superstitions. You'll know what questions to ask and how to use resources to find the truth. This book will also help prevent you from being taken advantage of by people who want to scam you.

So, grab that brain of yours and get ready for a wild ride into that wonderful, but far-from-perfect organ that makes life possible . . . and oh, so interesting.

CHAPTER 1

10 Reasons Not to Trust Your Brain

Our brains are obsessed with lists.

Your brain gets happy if you see a magazine cover that says, "5 Cool Ways to Exercise While You Eat Ice Cream" or "13 Dorky Dances Your Cat Will Love." What's so special about lists? Our brains are constantly hit with tons and tons of random information that overwhelm us with choices. So a list makes us think, "Phew! At least something is organized." A list soothes our brains by telling us the world isn't so chaotic. Also, a list organizes information into smaller chunks, so we can stop, focus, and mentally digest what is being presented.

Here's a list that might not calm your brain, though. That's because it summarizes the ways your brain can't be trusted.

1. It is overconfident.

When we make a mistake, such as tripping on some stairs and failing a math test, our brains will do everything they can to show us that the reason is NOT us, of course. Our brains never like admitting when we do something dumb.

2. Its memories are often sketchy.

We like to think that our brains are perfect video recorders that capture all our experiences perfectly. Nope. The truth is that memories are actually built by our brains. We frequently recall wrong information that we believe it is true. ("But I did put the toilet seat down, I swear.")

3. It is fooled by authority and fame.

If you see a famous athlete wearing a particular brand of shoes, you're more likely to beg your parents to buy them. Our brains will even do things that are harmful to us, such as buying clothing we cannot afford, if we think someone "important" is telling us to do them.

4. It thinks the world is always a fair place.

Our minds are wired to think that life is fair. Good actions are always rewarded, and bad ones are always punished. We like to think that if something bad happens to someone, they obviously deserved it. Scientists call this idea the "Just-World Hypothesis."

5. It tells us we're great at multitasking.

Some people brag that they can do lots of things at once—and do them all well. The brain is not designed that way. When we try to multitask, we get more stressed, more distracted, and make more mistakes. For example, when adults try to talk on the phone, eat french fries, and scratch a hard-to-reach itch at the same time, it can lead to disaster.

6. It loves to make connections even when there aren't any.

Our brains are pattern-making machines. Much of the time, this ability helps us draw observations and solve problems. But we often go overboard. For example, someone who buys a lottery ticket with the numbers of their birthday might think their "luck" caused them to win the jackpot. In truth, it was just a coincidence.

7. It distorts information.

We only see what we want to see. We like when the world supports what we believe. When we encounter some information that completely goes against our beliefs, our brains ignore it. And when we come across information that sort of supports our beliefs, we exaggerate it so that it is proof that we're totally right about everything all the time. Imagine you wear a pair of green socks before an important race. When you do well, your brain convinces you that the socks had something to do with your victory.

8. It is scared of new things.

The brain is comforted by the familiar. So we'll stick with habits that aren't good for us just because we already know them. This explains why we sometimes stay with friends even though they are mean to us. It's also why we eat the same brand of breakfast cereal every day. It takes a lot of effort to get us out of our comfort zones.

9. It is often lazy when solving problems.

When we have to solve a problem, we usually don't like taking a long time thinking of a solution. When we're doing homework, for example, we don't want to look at each problem from many angles. Our brains are eager to find fast, easy answers so we can move onto more important activities such as taking a nap.

10. It is swayed by emotions, so we sometimes make poor decisions.

Humans are social beings, and we like to fit in with others. Advertisers know this, so they use visual tricks to make us buy new products we might not have bought if we were less concerned about what others think. Teenagers are much more likely to be swayed by their amygdalas (see page 15), which control emotions, than by their frontal cortex, which helps control wild, possibly dangerous actions.

Breaking Down Your Brain
A Tour Inside Your Noggin

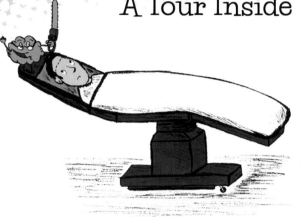

It's time to get inside your head. Once we get beyond your stylish haircut and that pesky skull, we arrive at the warm, pink, mushy thing that looks sort of like a cauliflower. In other words, your brain! In this chapter, we're going to explore the important parts of this organ and find out what makes it tick.

The Cerebrum

This big, jiggly part of the brain is the *cerebrum* (suh-REE-brum), which in Latin means "brain." The cerebrum gives you the power to think brilliant thoughts and stores all your most treasured memories. This part is also to blame for making stupid, bone-headed decisions, and storing your most embarrassing moments. The cerebrum is divided into two halves called *hemispheres*, connected with a bridge of nerves. Here's something weird: The left hemisphere of your brain controls the right side of your body, and vice versa. The outer layer of the cerebrum is called the *cerebral cortex*, nicknamed the "gray matter." The cerebrum is made of four areas called *lobes*. Each lobe does a different job.

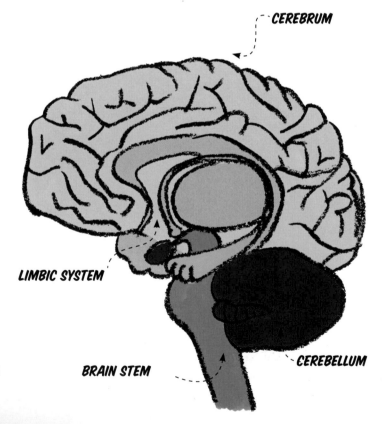

CEREBRUM

LIMBIC SYSTEM

BRAIN STEM

CEREBELLUM

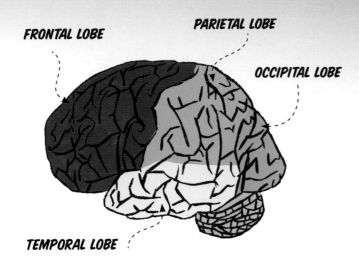

FRONTAL LOBE

PARIETAL LOBE

OCCIPITAL LOBE

TEMPORAL LOBE

Frontal Lobe

The *frontal lobe* controls thinking, talking, planning, organizing, solving problems, and paying attention. When you decide to make deliberate movements, such as hopping on one foot and scratching your nose, your frontal lobe runs the show. This is also where your "personality" lives and determines behavior such as if you're outgoing or shy.

Parietal Lobe

The *parietal lobe* monitors and controls body movement, controls visual functions such as reading, and processes information about your senses, especially touch. If you touch something, this lobe gathers information about temperature, pressure, and pain. When your tongue tastes, the information is sent to this lobe, so you know whether to say, "Yum" or "Yuck."

Occipital Lobe

The *occipital lobe* controls information about vision. Information from your eyes is compared here with images stored in your memories. What you see isn't always what you get, as you'll find out in Chapter 3.

Temporal Lobe

This is where memories are made. This lobe interprets sounds, music, language, and recognizes objects, such as faces. The part of this lobe called the *hippocampus* plays a role in storing memories.

The Cerebellum

Next up is the *cerebellum* (sare-uh-BELL-um), which means "little brain" in Latin. It is located just below the rear part of the cerebrum. The cerebellum's job is to control all your movements—everything from snapping your fingers to balancing on a skateboard. When you trip and face-plant in front of your secret crush, blame your cerebellum.

Fun Fact
Your whole brain makes up less than 2 percent of your body weight, but it uses about 20 percent of your body's oxygen.

The Limbic System

Below the cerebrum are a group of structures known as the *limbic system*. This system controls our feelings, memories, and learning. The limbic system is nicknamed "the lizard brain" because it is these parts of your mind that sometimes let emotions run wild and control your thoughts. Your cerebrum sees a bake sale and thinks, "I won't ruin my dinner by eating a bunch of brownies." Your limbic system jumps in and says, "Forget that, cerebrum! Me want brownies, NOW!"

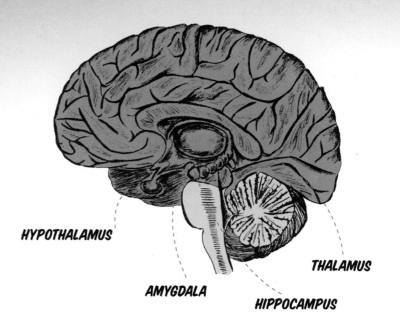

HYPOTHALAMUS

AMYGDALA

THALAMUS

HIPPOCAMPUS

> **Here, with their fancy Greek names, are the main parts of the limbic system.**

Thalamus
(means "inner room")
Everything you see, hear, taste, and touch comes to this part of the brain first. (Smells go to other areas of the brain.) Your thalamus helps you focus your attention on one activity and block the others out.

Hypothalamus
(means "under the inside room")
This part collects information about functions inside you, such as body temperature, sleepiness, and whether you're hungry or thirsty.

Hippocampus
(means "sea horse")
Memories are made here. This part collects information from the working memory in the cerebrum and uses electrical signals and chemicals to store them. As you might have guessed, it's shaped like a sea horse.

Amygdala
(means "almond")

This is the part of the brain that controls emotions, especially fear. Because of the way we're hardwired, we often feel panic, even if there's no real threat. Scientists call this "fight or flight" syndrome.

The Brain Stem

Finally, there's your brainstem, the tube-like chunk at the base of your brain. This part is in charge of keeping you alive, so don't make fun of it. Without your brain stem, you wouldn't be able to breathe, have your heart beat, digest food, or control your body temperature.

Neurons

So how many parts make up your brain? Not five, not one hundred, not a million. Try about 86 billion. That's the number of nerve cells that make up your brain. These cells, called *neurons*, are so small you need a microscope to see them.

A small group of them look like the image on the right.

Neurons are a very chatty bunch. They use chemicals and electricity to send trillions of signals to each other. The more you do a particular action, the smoother these connections become. When you learn to bike, the neurons have to build their network of connections little by little. But once you're a two-wheeling pro, these neuron communications becomes automatic.

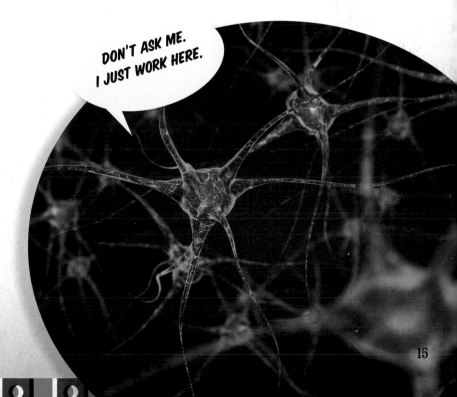

DON'T ASK ME. I JUST WORK HERE.

Total Truth or Phony Fact?

Before delving any further into that fascinating brain of yours, it's time for a quiz that will give your Baloney Detector a quick workout. Your Baloney Detector (BD) are those parts of your brain that decide if weird and wacky information is the truth or not. If your BD is strong, you're great at what scientists call *"critical thinking."* You can sniff out facts from fiction. But if your BD is iffy, then it's easy to pull the wool over your eyes. For tips on improving your BD, turn to page 76.

Grab a piece of paper and write down whether you think the following statements are true or false. The answers are upside down at the bottom of the next page.

1. In the Supreme Court building in Washington, D.C., there's a basketball court. It's known as "The Highest Court in the Land."

2. If you swallow chewing gum, it takes seven years to digest it.

3. Scientists have found proof that the T. rex's closest living relative is a chicken.

4. A penny dropped from the Empire State Building can kill a person on the ground.

5. The astronauts who visited the moon left behind about a hundred bags of poop, pee, and puke.

6. In Japan, letting a sumo wrestler make your baby cry is considered good luck.

7. If you leave a tooth in a cup of cola overnight, by morning the tooth will be completely dissolved.

9. There are more nerve connections (synapses) in your brain than there are stars in the universe.

8. Humans only use 10 percent of their brain.

10. A British man named Tim Price changed his name to Tim Pppppppppprice to make it more difficult for telemarketers to pronounce.

Answers: 1. True; 2. False; 3. True; 4. False; 5. True; 6. True; 7. False; 8. False; 9. False; 10. True

CHAPTER 3

Fool Your Eyes

Do you believe that seeing is believing?

In other words, can we trust our sense of vision? Much of the time, yes, but our eyes aren't 100 percent trustworthy. As optical illusions show, what we think we see isn't always the case. Actually, optical illusions are misnamed. They really trick our brains, not our eyes. In fact, scientist Neil deGrasse Tyson once joked that instead of calling them optical illusions, we should call them "brain failures."

Turning the Tables

Look at these two tables. Which surface do you think is longer: A or B?

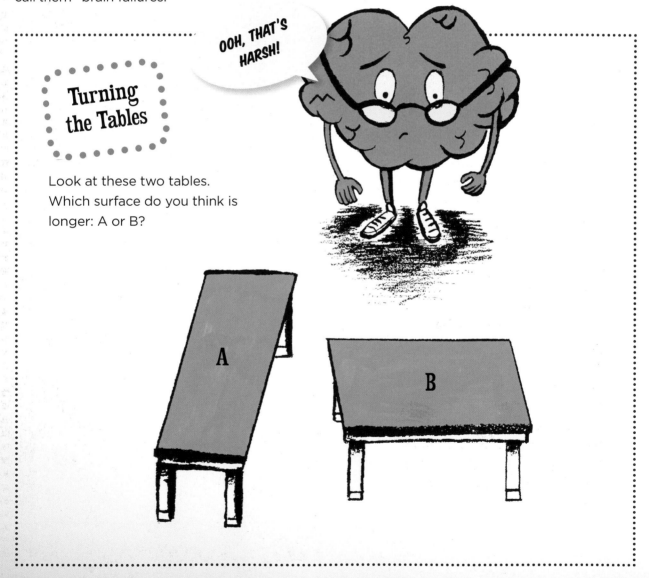

18

Once you've made your decision, measure both tables with a ruler. Were you surprised to find that both tabletops are the same size? If you cover the legs of each table, does the optical illusion still work as well?

What's Going On?

This illusion, created by psychologist Roger Shepard, shows that our minds have difficulty making sense of two-dimensional (2D) images that look three dimensional (3D). The occipital lobe of your cerebrum is what is tricked by this illusion.

Our brains think that items that are farther away (like the far end of table A) are smaller than items that appear closer (like the side edges of table B). Also, this illusion works because our brains are fooled by parallel lines. When parallel lines are vertical (table A), they often appear longer than if they're horizontal (table B). The slight diagonal angle of table A helps, too.

The Power of Stripes

Many people believe that if you want to look thinner than you are, you should wear clothes with vertical stripes. Some British psychologists put this idea to the test—and it's totally wrong. They dressed up female models in either horizontal striped dresses or vertical striped dresses. They discovered that people thought that when models wore the horizontal striped dress, they looked thinner.

Crazy Candles

Now that you know your eyes can't always trust your brain, let's try another one. Look at this birthday cake and pick which of the three layers is the same size as the thick candle on top? Don't measure them yet.

Which layer did you pick? Measure them with a ruler to find out.

The answer is the top layer is the same size as the candle. Once again, the reason this optical illusion works is because your brain is a ridiculously unreliable organ.

I'M NOT UNRELIABLE!

What's Going On?

This illusion shows that our minds tend to think of vertical shapes as being longer than horizontal ones. We overestimate the length of the vertical rectangle and underestimate the length of the horizontal one.

Why? First, our eyes can take in horizontal shapes more easily than vertical ones, and second, the vertical shape breaks the horizontal shape below it into two smaller parts.

Try looking at this illusion with only one eye and see if the effect is as strong. Most people find it is not.

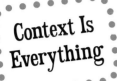

Context Is Everything

Whenever we look at something, we can't help looking at things nearby it. If a tall person stands next to a VERY tall person, they appear shorter than if they were standing next to a shorter person. In other words, context is everything.

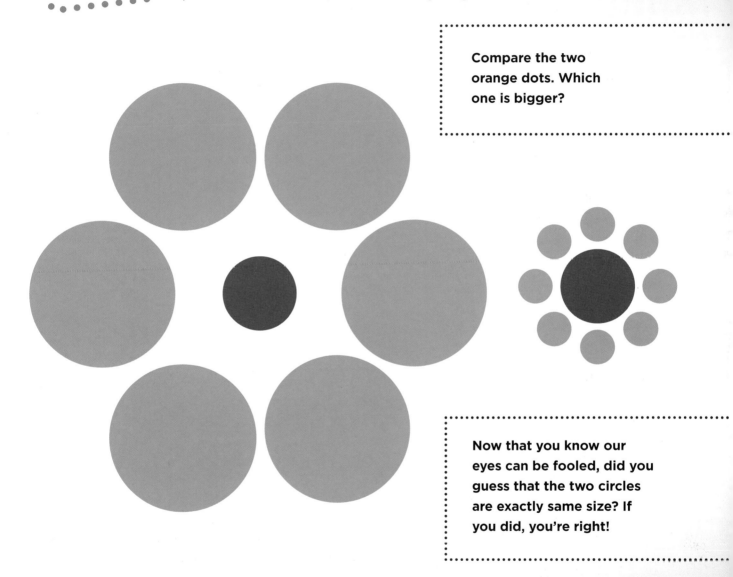

Compare the two orange dots. Which one is bigger?

Now that you know our eyes can be fooled, did you guess that the two circles are exactly same size? If you did, you're right!

Hermann Ebbinghaus, the German psychologist who discovered this illusion, explained that the size of the surrounding circles persuades our brains to think that the circle in the middle is either larger or smaller. The fact that both sets of surrounding circles are the same color makes our brains think they are somehow related. Also, the distance between the orange circle and the blue ones around it is different. More space around the circle makes it appear smaller, and vice versa.

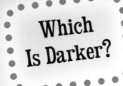

Which Is Darker?

Look at the picture below and describe the colors of the A part and B part. Which is darker?

What's Going On?

If you put your finger over the border between A and B, you'll see that they are both the exact same shade of gray!

Each of the gray areas looks different because of what's near them, and how they appear to be lit. When we look at this two-dimensional image, we imagine that it is three dimensional because of the shadows. If you look at the shadow, where do you think the light is coming from? The upper right. Our brain tells us the top square is lit, and the bottom one is in the shadow. In other words, the top square looks darker than it really is, and the bottom one seems lighter than it really is.

Online Trickery

Do an Internet search for "pink dots illusion" and you'll discover a cool video about changing colors. Stare at the "x" in the middle as the pink dots swirl around. Your brain will think it sees a green dot traveling around the circle. To find out how it works, look up "Troxler's fading."

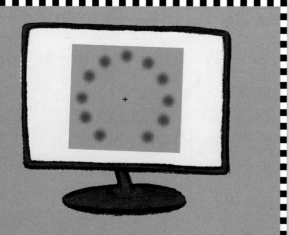

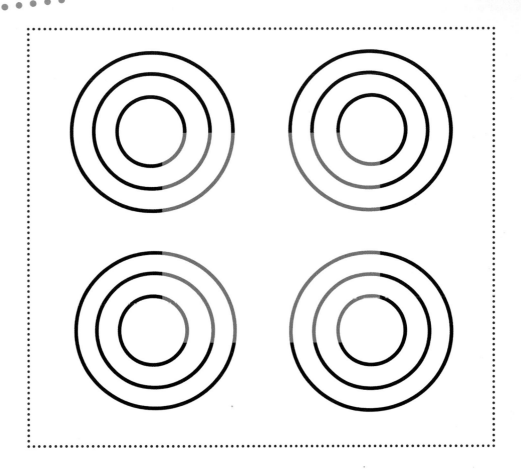

Blue Square

Here's another illusion that uses color to trick our mind. View it in bright light. Look at the light blue square in the middle of this picture. Pay special attention to the edges of the blue square between the circles.

What's Going On?

Use your hand to cover up the bottom two circles. What happens to the middle edges of the square? They disappear! That's because it was never there to begin with. Our brains love to fill in gaps. So, as long as there were parts of a square, our brain saw the whole thing.

Mind-Bending Motion

Sometimes your brain can be tricked into thinking that still objects are moving.

Stare at the black dot for a few seconds, and then move your head back and forth toward and away from the page. What do you see?

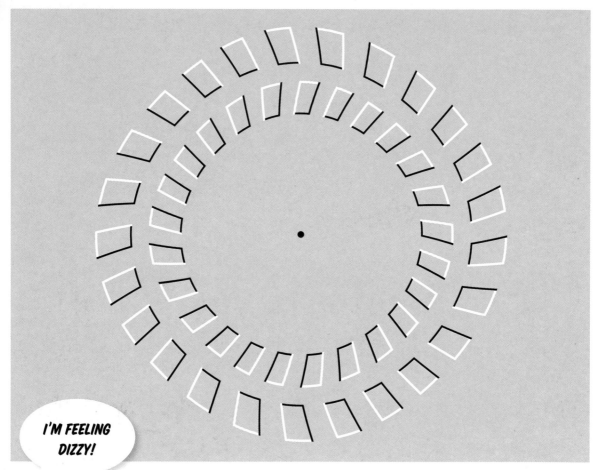

I'M FEELING DIZZY!

What's Going On?

Most people see the circles rotating in different directions. The scientists who discovered this illusion explained that this trick only works in your *peripheral vision*. This type of vision is what your eyes see off to the sides.

If you look carefully at the shapes that make up the circles in the picture, you can see that the shadows on the circles are on opposite sides for different circles, so the circles move in opposite directions.

Coiling Snakes

Let your eyes wander over this wavy pattern. Does it appear to move? Now try this: If you block out a small section of this picture with your hands and stare at it—the motion stops!

What's Going On?

To find out, neuroscientists studied the eye movements of a group of volunteers. The scientists discovered that when the volunteers looked at this illusion and it appeared to move, their eyes made tiny, fast movements called *saccades*. We think we can hold our eyes perfectly still—but they are always making tiny movements. Some scientists explain that when you let your eyes wander around this illusion, your brain gets overloaded and thinks the picture is moving rather than your eyes.

Upside Down Is Not Right

Scientists have discovered that certain areas in our brains "light up" when we look at faces. But when we look at pictures upside down, we are sometimes fooled. Here's a photo of a woman.

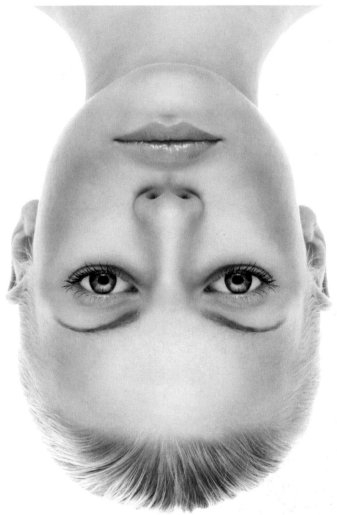

What's Going On?

What do you think you'll see when you flip it over? Try it! This illusion works for a few reasons. The first is that our brains are programmed to instantly recognize faces right-side up. When a face is flipped, we can't process it as quickly. Also, when we look at a normal face, our brain takes in the individual face pieces before we put them together—like pieces of a puzzle. Since the face parts are in the right location, we don't notice that the eyes and mouth are flipped from the rest of the photo. This effect was discovered by Peter Thompson in 1980 and has been dubbed the "Thatcher effect," since the first photo Thompson used was that of the British Prime Minister, Margaret Thatcher.

Funky Faces

Have you ever looked at a full moon and seen a face? Some people claim to see human faces in cinnamon buns, tortillas, and spills on the ground. How quickly can you find the faces in these photos? Really fast, right?

What's Going On?

The human brain—the hippocampus in the temporal lobe, to be specific—is remarkably good at identifying faces. We are hardwired to seek out eyes, noses, and mouths—even when they're not really there.

You can fool your brain into seeing spooky images that aren't really there. Try this example.

Stare at the dot on the girl's nose for 30 to 45 seconds. Then look to the white box underneath the image. Blink your eyes quickly. What do you see?

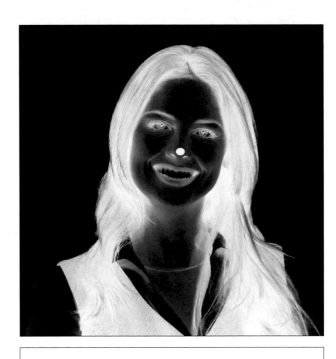

What's Going On?

This illusion is called a "negative afterimage" and is caused by special cells called *photoreceptors* at the back of your eyeballs. By staring at the dots on her nose, we slow down the normal jumpy micro saccades (see page 25) that happen when we look around. After 30 to 45 seconds of staring, some of the photoreceptor cells become overloaded and don't work properly. So other photoreceptors —especially those involved with color vision—are still fresh. So they fill in. They send out signals that are the same as if we were looking at the opposite colors. The brain thinks these signals are the opposite colors and creates a photo.

Wacky Words

Try this challenge. Grab some markers and a piece of white paper. Write down these color names in the following way:

> **Green:** with a red marker
> **Red:** with a blue marker
> **Orange:** with a green marker
> **Yellow:** with a black marker
> **Purple:** with an orange marker
> **Black:** with a yellow marker
> **Blue:** with a pink marker

Once you are done, as fast as you can, read aloud the **COLOR NAMES** of the words. Ignore the actual words, just say their color.

How did it go? Pretty slow, right?! This slowing down is called the "Stroop effect," after John Ridley Stroop, the psychologist who discovered it. Reading words is much more automatic for our brains than naming the color of letters.

Can you make sense of the following?

Aoccdrnig to a rscheearch at Cmabrigde Uinervtisy, it deosn't mttaer in waht oredr the ltteers in a wrod are, the olny iprmoetnt tihng is taht the frist and lsat ltteer be at the rghit pclae. The rset can be a total mses and you can sitll raed it wouthit a porbelm. Tihs is bcuseae the huamn mnid deos not raed ervey lteter by istlef, but the wrod as a wlohe. Amzanig huh?

Did you have any trouble reading it? Now, we're not sure if there really was any research done at Cambridge University about this, but it's fun!

What's Going On?

Your brain often saves time and energy by looking at the "big picture" rather than the itty bitty details. That's why you can read a paragraph in which only the first and last letters of the words are in the proper order.

Here are some quotes by famous people that are also misspelled.
See if you can figure out what they say. Answers on page 79.

"Imganiatoin is mroe ipmortnat
tahn knwoledge.
– ALBERT EINSTEIN

You msut od the tihngs yuo
htikn you cnanot od.
– ELEANOR ROOSEVELT

"I spnet msot of ym time
in shcool dadyreamnig
and mnaaged ot tunr
it into a livign."
– GEORGE LUCAS

"I usde to thnik the brian wsa the msot wondreflu orgna ni my bdoy.
Then I reailezd woh was tleling me thsi!"

– EMO PHILIPS

The huamn rbain has 100 bililon neuorns, each nueron conencted to
10 thosuand ohter neruons. Stitnig on yuor shouledrs is teh msot
copmlicated oejcbt in the kwonn uivrsene.

– MICHIO KAKU

Now cmoe up wtih yuor onw to smutp yuor fdreins!

Your eyes aren't the only senses that fool your brain! Turn the page to
find some ways to trick your ears, nose, tongue, and skin.

CHAPTER 4

Tricking Your Other Senses

As you saw in the last chapter, you can't always trust your eyes!

WELL, AT LEAST WE CAN TRUST OUR OTHER SENSES, RIGHT?

Nope. Sorry, Brian.

Our ears, nose, tongue, and skin usually do a great job telling us about the world around us. But, as you'll see, our brains can also be fooled by sounds, smells, tastes, and touch sensations. When you try the activities in this chapter, you'll find out that our senses often need one another to work properly.

OK, SMELL YA LATER!

Fool Your Ears

Our ears work by picking up vibrations in the air, which our brain then translates into sounds. But, like it or not, your ears and brain can't always be trusted. Your ears rely on shortcuts to handle the blizzard of sounds that hit you every day. These shortcuts sometimes backfire and give you bogus info. Your ears can trick you because they rely too much on the other senses, such as sight, to make sense of sounds around you. Just like there are optical illusions that fool your eyes, *auditory illusions* can baffle your ears.

Throw Your Voice

Ventriloquists (ven-TRIL-o-kwists) are entertainers who trick our brains by making us think that a puppet they're holding (called a "dummy") can actually talk. Of course, the ventriloquist is really creating the funny voice. But we fall for this illusion for three reasons:

1. The ventriloquist doesn't move his or her lips when the puppet talks. Our brains are pretty terrible at figuring out exactly where sounds come from. Think about when you watch a video on a computer or TV. We imagine the voices are coming out of the characters' mouths, rather than the truth—the voices are coming from the speakers on the side of the device. To keep their lips still when the puppet "talks," ventriloquists use a technique called *sound substitution*. More on this on page 35.

2. The cortex is the last stop on the sight-and-sounds train. Before then, your eyes see the puppet's mouth moving, at the same time your ears hear the ventriloquist's funny voice talking. Our cortex automatically assumes the sounds are coming from the puppet's mouth.

3. Ventriloquists misdirect our attention. They look directly at the puppet's eyes when it is "speaking," and they usually give the puppet a funny voice. In addition, by having the puppet character misbehave, the ventriloquist distracts us and supports the illusion that the puppet is a separate person.

Put on a Show

Becoming a top-notch ventriloquist takes many years of practice. You can still have fun trying the basics, and with practice, fool your friends and family.

What You Need
- A simple puppet that can move its mouth (or a sock)
- Mirror

What You Do

1. Experiment with the art of sound substitution. Hold your pointer in "Shhh!" position in front of your lips, and slowly say the alphabet. What letters can you say without moving your lips?

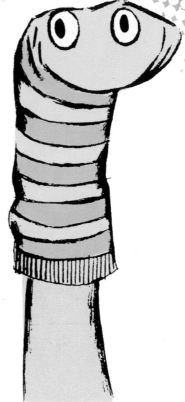

2. You'll find that you can say most letters easily except these six: B, F, M, P, V, and W. The secret to saying these six tricky letters is to actually say a different letter that sounds sort of the same. For example, when a ventriloquist says "B" they actually say "D." The sentence "Buy a big banana" becomes "Dy a Dig Danana." At first, this substitution won't sound right; but with practice, "D" can be made to sound like "B." One tip is to *think* the "B" sound when you *say* "D."

3. Here are the substitutions for the other five letters:
* For F, say "eth"
* For M, say "N"
* For P, say "T"
* For V, say "thee"
* For W, say "O+I"

4. Look in the mirror and say the whole alphabet again using the substitutions. It helps if you smile, so your lips are naturally apart. Next, try saying the alphabet in a funny voice—one that has a higher or lower pitch than yours.

5. Finally, put on a show with your puppet. Remember to argue with the puppet. This is a fun and effective distraction.

Torture Your Tongue

Practicing ventriloquism can give your tongue a workout. So do tongue twisters. Sure, there are the classics: "She sells seashells by the seashore" and "Toy boat, toy boat, toy boat." If you really want to tangle your tongue, try to say this wacky mouthful, as fast as you can, five times in a row.

"Pad kid poured curd pulled cod."

Don't feel bad if you can't do it. Scientists at the Massachusetts Institute of Technology (MIT) experimented with a number of sound combinations until they found the ones that cause our brains to freeze up.

KAD PID POURED...ACK!

Sound Illusions

Since this book can't make sounds (unless you drop it on the floor), use a computer to experience the sounds in these activities. But first, here are some terms to be familiar with:

Frequency: How quickly sound waves travels through the air
Pitch: The sound produced, based on its frequency
Notes: The group of pitches, in order, that makes musical scales
Octave: A series of eight notes, when two notes have a similar sound but one is higher or lower than the original note

Hearing with Your Eyes

How does what we see affect what we hear? We think we hear with our ears, but our eyes also play a role. Search online for a video of "The McGurk Effect." You'll see a person making the nonsense sound "bah, bah, bah." Then you'll see the same person appear to say "fah, fah, fah," "vah, vah, vah," or "gah, gah, gah." However, the person is really still saying "bah, bah, bah." You'll discover that the position of a person's mouth can make us think we're hearing things that aren't really there.

A Pitch Paradox

Does where you grew up affect how you hear musical pitches? Gather some friends or family members, and search online for "Tritone Paradox audio." Together you'll hear a series of four pairs of notes. As they listen, ask each person to decide if the pairs of notes go "down up" or "up down." Listen to these notes a second time if you want.

There is no right or wrong answer because all the computer-generated tones have more than one note played, an octave apart. So, both "down up" and "up down" are correct. Here's the weird part. The scientist found that people from California heard different pitch patterns than people from England did.

Up and Up and Up

Is it possible for the pitch of a sound to rise higher and higher forever? Your brain thinks so. Search online for "Shepard Tone" and listen to the audio or video file. The sounds you hear are mixed in a sneaky way: As the pitch appears to rise, new notes, an octave apart in the lower range, are slowly faded in. At the same time, notes an octave higher are slowly faded out. This keeps the average frequency the same, but creates the illusion that the sound is rising forever. This sound illusion is nicknamed the "audio barber pole" because like the barber shop pole illusion, the stripes make it look like there's continuous upward movement.

Warped Waves?

Have you ever noticed that when a fire engine races by you, its siren sound seems to drop in pitch as it passes you? The same goes for a car racing by honking its horn. Search online for "Doppler Effect" to hear some examples. (It's named after Christian Doppler, the scientist who discovered it.) What's going on? The fire truck's siren gives off sound waves. As it moves forward, the sound waves bunch up in the front and spread out behind it. When you watch a fire truck come toward you, these bunched-up sound waves sound like a higher pitch. When the truck drives away from you, the spread-out sound waves make your ears hear a lower sound. If you were riding on the fire truck, you'd hear a steady sound that neither rises or falls.

LONG WAVELENGTH/ LOW FREQUENCY

SMALL WAVELENGTH/ HIGH FREQUENCY

Fool Your Nose and Tongue

Did you ever wonder why your favorite foods taste bland when you have a cold?

That's because our sense of smell and sense of taste are closely related. When you eat, your brain gets signals from both your taste buds and your nose.

YOU MIGHT THINK IT'S FUN TO EAT WITH A RUNNY NOSE, BUT IT'S NOT! GET IT?

Mystery Beans

To explore the connection between our senses of smell and taste, try this experiment.

What You Need
- Big bag of mini jelly beans, assorted flavors
- Blindfold (for each person), could be a scarf tied around eyes
- 10 paper cups, numbered 1 to 10
- Pen
- Water for cleaning out mouth
- Piece of paper with this chart

Jelly Bean Numbers	Guess # 1 (Pinching nose with blindfold on)	Guess # 2 (Nose open with blindfold on)	Guess # 3 (With no with blindfold or nose pinching)

What You Do

1. With a friend, sort the jelly beans into 10 cups, each cup containing at least 3 of the same flavor jelly bean. Try to pick a variety of jellybean flavors: some sweet, some sour.

2. Have your friend put on a blindfold on and mix up the order of the cups. Then label each cup 1 to 10, and put the cups in a line.

3. Have your friend hold his or her nose closed, still with the blindfold on. One by one, give your friend a jelly bean from one of the cups starting with cup 1. Ask him to try to guess what flavor jelly bean it is. You can help your friend by telling him the choices. Every time your friend makes a guess, write it down on the chart.

4. Have your friend remove his fingers from his nose, but keep the blindfold on. Then repeat what you did in Step 3. Write down his 10 guesses again on the chart.

5. Finally, repeat the process one more time, but let your friend taste the jelly beans without the blindfold and without holding his nose.

6. Look at the chart and see how removing the senses of sight and smell affected your friend's ability to identify the jelly bean flavor. Repeat the whole experiment, but this time, switch roles.

Making Sense of Scents

Food companies know that the more appealing their product sounds, the more likely you are to buy it. That's why when you walk through the supermarket, your eyes are drawn to certain packages. Some scientists wanted to find out if the very same odor could be appealing or appalling—depending on the label. The answer has to do with our brains. In particular, our expectations can affect our taste buds. Try a similar experiment with your friends to find out for yourself.

What You Need
- 2 volunteers
- Blindfolds
- Small shallow cups
- Small amounts of grated parmesan cheese and cumin

What to Do

1. Place the cheese and cumin in separate cups.

2. Ask your two volunteers to put on blindfolds, and tell them you're going to put different smells under their noses. Do not let them see the containers with the smelly substances. Tell them not to sniff too hard but just to get the aroma of each smell.

3. Start with the cheese. Tell your first volunteer that this is something you might put on pizza. Let him smell it. Then tell the second volunteer that the this is something you might smell if someone felt nauseated. Have them rate the smells on a scale of 1 to 5, with 5 being the most appealing. Repeat the process with the second smell. Tell the first volunteer, "This is something you might have in Indian food." Tell the second volunteer,

"This is a smell you might find on dirty clothes." Again, have them rate the smell on a scale of 1 to 5.

4. Repeat with other smelly substances around the home, such as perfume, garlic, onions, and pinecones.

5. When they are done, reveal that they both smelled the same two aromas. Did the setup for each sniffing experience affect the rating?

Flower Power

When you walk into a room that smells of freshly baked cookies, you will be in a better mood than if you walk into one that smells like dirty diapers. Scientists wondered if smells could affect how trustworthy people feel. They set up an experiment with 90 people. Half went into a room that smelled of lavender, a soothing aroma. The other half went into a room scented with peppermint, which is known for making people feel energetic.

Then the 90 people played a trust game. In this game, one person is given money, which they can keep or give away. When they gave away the money, the scientists tripled it. The person who got all this money then decided if they wanted to share any of their money. Those who smelled lavender gave away more money than did those who smelled peppermint.

Sweet and Sour

How does the temperature of something you eat or drink affect its taste? Try this simple experiment to find out. Take two small pieces of sweet food and two pieces of sour food. The food could be two kinds of candy or two contrasting foods, such as a sweet apple and a slice of lemon. First, hold an ice cube on your tongue for one minute, and then taste the sweet food item. Then take a drink of water to clean your tongue and repeat this process with the sour food item. Then take another drink of water and wait for your tongue to return to normal temperature. Now taste the two foods and compare the experience with your "frozen tongue" test. Did the food taste different? How so?

All Hot Chocolate Tastes the Same?

Hot chocolate tastes the same no matter what color cup you drink it in, right? Not so fast. Some scientists in Europe put this question to the test. They asked sixty people to rate hot chocolate that was served in four different colored plastic cups: white, cream, orange, and red. (The cups were all white on the inside.) They found people said the hot chocolate was tastier and sweeter when it was served in the orange- and cream-colored cups.

Fool Your Skin

Your skin can feel pressure, pain, vibration, and temperature. Most of the time, our skin does a super job of helping us make sense of the world. But not always. Grab a friend and try out these short experiments.

Wait, That's MY Finger?

Press your hand against a friend's hand, like in the illustration on the right. Then, with your other hand, gently stroke both of your pointer fingers. Feels weird, huh? That's because when you touch the other person's finger, you are only feeling a one-way sensation, but when you touch your own finger at the same time, your brain is confused. It doesn't expect to feel one of the two fingers in the pair.

Magic String

Have your friend hold out and clasp her hands together, with her pointer fingers sticking out, about an inch apart. Tell her you have an invisible string that you're going to wrap around her fingers. Pretend to wind it around and around her finger—then pull tight. Do this a few times, and see if your friend's fingers start to pull together. Sometimes this "invisible string" works because of the power of suggestion.

Pretend Egg Crack

Have a friend sit in a chair facing away from you. Tell them you are going to put various objects on their hand, and they have to guess what they are. Use three SAFE random objects, such as a stuffed animal, a rubber ball, a comb, and so on. Show them the item after they make their guess to see if they're right. Then tell them the next item will make their hair look beautiful. Make a fist, and lightly tap the bony part of your hand twice on their head, and ask if they know what it is. Say, "I'll try again!" Repeat the tapping and say, "Oh, no, the egg broke!" As you say this, gently slide your fingers down the back of the friend's neck to create the illusion of an egg running down. You can enhance this illusion by secretly dipping your hand in a cup of cold water beforehand so your fingertips are a little wet.

You're Getting Warmer...or Is That Colder?

Get three bowls, one with hot (not dangerously hot) water, one with icy-cold water, and one with warm water. Put the warm water bowl in the middle of the other two. Then stick one hand in the hot water, and the other in the freezing cold water. Hold them there for one minute. Then, take both hands out at the same time, and put them in the bowl of warm water. What does it feel like? Each hand won't be able tell the real temperature of the warm water because our skin cells can get used to a certain temperature and take time to adjust to a new one.

Two Fingers, Two Noses

Cross your pointer and middle fingers, and then gently rub them up and down your nose, so that each side of each finger is touching your nose. Keep it up for about 30 to 45 seconds, and your fingertips will feel as though you have two noses! (It can help to close your eyes to focus on your skin sensations.) That's because you're the edges of your fingers aren't used to touching one object because they are on opposite sides.

Crawling Fingers

Ask a friend to put her bent arm on a table, so that the crook of her elbow is exposed. Tell her that you're going to ask her to close her eyes as you walk your fingers up her forearm. Her job is to say, "Now!" when she thinks you are just about to touch the crook of her elbow. Once she closes her eyes, put your pointer finger and middle finger on her wrist, and slowly walk your fingers side to side, gradually moving up her forearm. You'll both be surprised to find out that she'll say "Now!" long before you get to the crook of her elbow.

The Art of Pickpocketing

Pickpockets are remarkably good at distracting our brains, so they can steal our possessions. They can sneak our wallets, watches, and much more. Expert pickpocket entertainer Apollo Robbins was interviewed by neuroscientists for a fascinating book called *Sleights of Mind*. By talking with him and watching his masterful pickpocketing, they learned some of his secrets:

Peripheral Vision: Our eyes aren't that great at seeing objects off to the side. To test this, hold out an arm off to the side and stick out your thumb. Then very slowly move your arm until it is in front of your face. At what point during this movement can you see the tip of your thumb. Not until it is almost in front of your face, right? Pickpockets know that if they do some action in your peripheral vision, you probably won't see it.

Jumpy vs. Smooth Eye Movements: There are two main ways our eyes move.
(1) One is called *saccades*, in which our eyes dart about quickly, taking in a number of sights in a split second.

(2) The second type of eye movement is called *smooth pursuit*. This is when you track a moving object with your eyes. Look at a friend's eyes as you try this experiment. Hold up your two pointer fingers, and ask them to look from the left one to the right one, and back. You can see that your friend's eyes jump in saccades. But if you then ask your friend to follow your hand as it moves in an arc slowly through the air, you'll see their eyes move in smooth pursuit. So what does this have to do with pickpocketing? Read on!

Arches vs. Straight Lines: The human eye is more easily distracted by curved motion than by straight lines. So, if a pickpocket wants us to watch his hands, he moves them in an arch (which we follow in smooth pursuit) rather than straight across (which we follow through saccades).

Sensory Afterimage: You know how you feel like you're wearing a hat, long after you take it off? That's because of something called *sensory afterimage*. Pickpockets can use this knowledge when they steal watches. They squeeze the person's wrist briefly but leave the watch on. This makes the person's wrist slightly numb for a few seconds. When the pickpocket returns, he can remove the watch while the person is distracted.

CHAPTER 5

How Magicians Mess with Your Mind

Magicians seem to do the impossible.

They make doves appear out of thin air. They take two solid metal rings and—CLING!—link them together. They wave their hands to make people to vanish right. They even seem to read our minds.

Sure, magic tricks often use special props, but the most important secret that all magicians know is that our brains can be easily fooled. In this chapter, you'll learn some simple, cool tricks that you can use to fool your friends and family.

The Science of Magic

Before we get into the tricks, let's look at some ways that magicians mess with our heads.

The Illusion of Choice

When a magician says, "Pick a card, any card, then put it back into the deck," the magician gives us a false sense of freedom. We think he has given us control over the trick's outcome. Nothing could be further from the truth. As soon as we pick a card, the magician uses *sleight of hand* to get the card we selected exactly where he wants it. Sleight of hand happens when magicians secretly hide objects like coins in their hands, pretend to hold objects that aren't really there, or use their hands to direct our attention away from their sneaky moves. Often, a magician will "force" us to pick the exact card he wants, even though we think it is our choice.

Misdirection

We think we can focus on more than one thing at a time but we can't. Human attention is like a spotlight. If we focus on one object or event, we miss others nearby. If a magician wants us to look closely at her right hand, she will move it in a dramatic way, and follow her right hand with her eyes. Our brains are drawn to motion. While this is going on, the left hand is free to do sneaky things like hide an object they want to vanish.

WHO IS THAT LOOKING OVER YOUR SHOULDER? I WOULDN'T TURN AROUND IF I WERE YOU!!! NO, DON'T TURN AROUND! SEE WHAT I DID? I DISTRACTED YOU WHILE I TOOK YOUR WALLET! CHECK YOUR POCKET NOW. IT'S GONE, RIGHT?

Online Trickery

Search online for "invisible gorilla" and watch the video that asks you to count how many times the people in white pass the ball. This is an example of our brains focusing on something and missing others.

Laughter, Stories, and Goofs

The words a magician says when she does a trick is called *patter*. This patter is often silly because magicians know that if we're laughing, we're not paying careful attention to their secret moves. Stories are another great way to distract our brains, so we're wondering, "What happens next?" rather than "Why did he slip his hand in his pants pocket?" Another common brain trick that magicians pull is appearing to make a mistake. When a trick seems to have gone horribly wrong, our minds are so busy gloating, "Ha-ha! The magician goofed!" that we don't notice him pulling off the move that will make the trick turn out perfectly a moment later.

Change Blindness

When we look at something, our brains hold that picture in our mind for a few seconds. So even if the object changes slightly, we don't notice it. When a magician takes a coin in his right hand, and then presses it into his left and closes it, our minds aren't fast enough to realize that as soon as the coin touched his left hand, he quickly and skillfully pulled the coin back into his right hand.

Online Trickery

Search online for videos of "retention vanish" to see how a magician takes advantage of change blindness to make a coin disappear.

The Power of Patterns

Magicians know that our brains are pattern-making machines. Our minds are so pattern-obsessed that we'll jump to the wrong conclusion about how a trick works. A great example is when a magician pulls coins out of the air, and then tosses them into a bucket. (Do a web search for "Miser's Dream" to see examples of this trick.) Without giving away the secret of this trick, one thing to know is that when a magician pulls a bunch of coins out of the air, he doesn't use the same method every time. Just when we think we know how the magician does it, he switches to a different method. One time he might secretly remove some coins from his pocket, another time he might make us think he tossed a coin in the bucket—but really kept it in his hand for the next "appearance."

Double Matchmaker

This card trick gives the illusion that you can predict the future.

The Illusion

After your volunteer shuffles a deck of cards, fan them before you and remove two cards—your prediction cards—and put them facedown on the table. The volunteer then cuts the deck anywhere they want and places the two halves of the deck perpendicular to each other. You reveal the two cards where the volunteer cut the deck, then flip over your predictions. There are two matching pairs that share the same number and color.

The Secret

By misdirecting the volunteer's attention both visually and through patter, you fool them into thinking they selected two cards at random. The truth is you knew ahead of time which pair of cards the volunteer would select, so you could predict the matches at the start.

How You Do It

1. Ask the volunteer to shuffle the cards and then hand them to you.

2. Fan the cards in front of you, so the volunteer can't see them. Then casually look at the top and bottom cards. These will be the two cards that the volunteer will later think he picked. As you look through the cards in front of you, tell the volunteer, "I'm going to make two predictions." Find the matches for the top and bottom cards and put them face down next to each other on the table.

3. Place the deck on the table and ask the volunteer to cut the cards, removing a stack of cards from the top and setting them aside. Then have them pick up the remaining stack of cards and place them in a criss-cross pattern on top of the first pile. The two piles now look like a plus sign.

4. Make eye contact, and then summarize what has happened so far: "At the start of the trick, I made two predictions over here. Then, I asked you to cut the deck anywhere you wanted. You could have separated the deck at any point. I had no idea where you could cut the deck. Now, we're going to look at the two cards that you cut to." (Note: This patter is important for misdirection, so the volunteer isn't thinking clearly about the order of the two card piles.)

5. Say, "Let's look at the two cards you cut to." (This is a lie, but the passage of time and the crossing of the halves will fool the volunteer.) Lift the top half of cards and pull out the bottom card of this pile and put it face up on the table. Then put this pile down, and lift the top card of the bottom pile and place this face up on the table, next to the other face-up card.

6. Flip over the two prediction cards and show that they match the two cards that were predicted at the start.

⬤ **Black Magic**

Show your audience that you have the power to make someone else read your mind.

The Illusion

A table is filled with a bunch of random objects. One volunteer leaves the room, while another selects an object on the table. The first volunteer returns to the room and you use "the power of mind control" to help them identify which object was selected while he was out.

The Secret

The volunteer who leaves the room is actually a "stooge"—a secret magician's assistant. They know a simple but tricky secret code to tell which object is the selected one. The stooge knows that when the magician points to a black object, the very next object to be pointed to is the selected one.

How You Do It

1. Before the trick, place 10 to 20 objects on a table. At least three or four of them should be black or mostly black. Do this trick before an audience of at least three people; a larger group is even better.

2. Ask for a volunteer who will be receiving your magical mind-reading signals. Have that person either leave the room with another volunteer to make sure they aren't peeking. Ask another volunteer at the table to point to (or say aloud the name of) one of the objects on the table. It can be highly specific—such as a particular crayon in a box and a specific page number in a book. Then have the volunteer who left return to the room.

3. Explain to the returning volunteer that while he or she was out, another volunteer at the table selected one of the objects on the table. Say, "I will now use my powers of mind control to help you figure out which object it is."

4. One by one, you lift up an object on the table and ask the volunteer (stooge) if each object is the one the other volunteer selected. Just before you get to the correct answer, ask if one of the black objects is the choice. This will tip off the stooge that the very next object is the right one. (Note: If the volunteer happens to pick a black object, then the secret signal is picking a different black object just before picking the black one that was selected.)

Experiments in Mind Reading

If you think that reading someone else's mind is only possible in make-believe movies and magic shows, you're in for a surprise. Scientists at the University of Washington are doing experiments that use high-tech machines to reveal what our minds are thinking.

Every time we think, our brains create electric signals. These scientists are trying to figure out how we can use machines called *electroencephalograms (EEG)* to pick up and transmit these signals.

In one experiment, a person's head was attached to an EEG. The person was told to think of an animal. Then a person in another room typed some yes-no questions about the animal. If the first person thought "yes," their brain signal looked different than if they thought "no." By putting together the clues, the person in the other room could figure out the animal's identity most of the time.

You Choose Two, I Choose One

You and your volunteer take turns pulling objects off a table until there's one left—the one you predicted before the trick started!

The Illusion

A bunch of random objects are on a table. You show the volunteer a folded piece of paper with a prediction on it. You and the volunteer then take turns removing objects one at a time, until one object remains. You pull out an envelope and then dramatically open it. It contains a piece of paper with the prediction of the last object left.

The Secret

The volunteer only thinks they have free choice throughout the trick, but of course they don't. The rules of the game keep you in control and allow you to force the choice of the final object, so it will match your prediction. Also, the fact that the volunteer choose two and you choose only one makes the volunteer believe they have more control.

How You Do It

1. Before the trick: Gather an even number of random objects from around the house—between 10 and 20.

2. Select one of the objects and write it on a piece of paper, "I predict the object left on the table will be the _____." Seal the prediction in an envelope and put it on the corner of the table.

3. Explain the rules to the volunteer. First, she'll point to any two objects, and you remove one of them. Then, you switch roles. You'll point to two of the remaining objects, and the volunteer gets to remove one of them. You'll follow this pattern back and forth, until only one object is left on the table.

4. Follow this procedure, being careful to leave the predicted object on the table. Keep going until there is one object left.

5. Before opening the envelope, recap what happened. "We could have eliminated any object on the table, right? My prediction has been sitting there the whole time." Open the note and read the prediction—which will be correct!

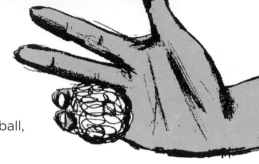

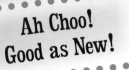

**Ah Choo!
Good as New!**

Using the power of magic,
you can rip up a tissue,
and instantly restore it.

The Illusion

Rip a tissue into pieces, squeeze the pieces together in a ball,
wave a straw over it, and—POOF!—it's whole again.

The Secret

As you might guess, there are actually two identical tissues used. The key is to
hide the second one, and then switch it with the ripped up one, which is then
secretly tossed.

How You Do It

1. Before you do the trick, take a tissue and crumble it into a small ball and put it inside
your right hand, hidden in your third and fourth fingers. Hold the other fingers as naturally as
possible, so they don't look suspicious.

2. With your left hand, reach across the table
to a tissue box and pull out one tissue. Pinch the
corners of the tissue with the thumb, pointer,
and middle fingers of each hand, so it is open in
front of the audience.

*THIS WILL ALSO MAKE THEIR
BRAINS THINK: "WELL, IF THE
LEFT HAND IS TOTALLY EMPTY,
IT CAN'T POSSIBLY BE HIDING
ANYTHING.*

3. Tear the tissue in pieces a few times. Then bunch all the pieces into a ball and squeeze it hard with your right hand (the hand that is hiding the tissue you crumbled in step 1). One at a time, stick your left thumb, pointer, and ring finger into the right fist to give the impression you are squashing the ripped paper ball even more. Show your empty left hand to the audience.

4. With your left hand, reach into your right hand and remove the non-torn crumbled ball you were hiding, while keeping the torn-up crumbled ball concealed in your right hand. You need to quickly pull the non-torn crumbled ball from the bottom of your fist to the top of the torn crumbled ball. Hold the non-torn ball of paper in your left hand, but pretend that no magic has happened yet! As you play around with the (non-torn) tissue ball, gently lifting tiny sections of the tissue, say things that suggest the ball is still torn up. "Okay, let's make sure all the little bits of tissue are pushed in." Squeeze this ball together again in the left hand.

5. Hold out the tissue near the spectator's face for them to blow on it. (Again, this creates the illusion that you aren't hiding anything.) After they blow on it, have them say, "Achoo! Kalamazoo!" Slowly unravel it. Position your hands the same way— with the fourth and fifth fingers of each hand pulled inward. (This creates a mirror image, so later when you open your hands fully, the spectator will think both hands have been empty all along.)

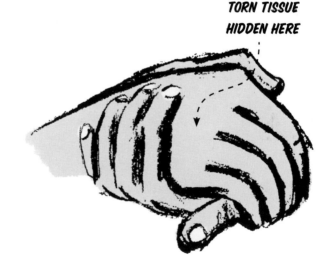

TORN TISSUE HIDDEN HERE

6. Little by little open the tissue so it is facing the spectator again. Use the left hand to hand the whole tissue to the spectator. While they look it over, you can quickly stash the torn-up tissue ball in your pocket.

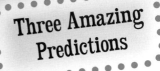

Three Amazing Predictions

The magician makes three incredible predictions about what a spectator will choose—and, at the end, each one is revealed to be correct!

The Illusion

The magician writes a secret prediction on a piece of paper, folds it, and puts it into a cup. Then the spectator is presented with a bunch of different colored crayons and told to pick one. The magician makes a second secret prediction, and puts it into the same cup. The spectator is asked to hold up any number of fingers between 1 and 10. Finally, the magician writes down a third secret prediction, and then asks the spectator to pick one of three coins on the table. Afterward, the magician reaches into the cup and reads the predictions aloud. Each one is correct!

The Secret

This trick uses two famous magician moves. The first is called the *one-ahead rule*. The magician's predictions are actually off by one, but the spectator doesn't know this because the predictions aren't revealed until the end. The second move is called the *magician's choice*: a kind of force where no matter what choice the volunteer makes, the result is what the magician wanted. Details on each are below.

How You Do It

1. Before the trick, gather these supplies: table, plastic cup that you can't see through, stack of small pieces of paper (all the same size and color) a pen, 5 to 10 different colored crayons, 3 coins (such as a quarter, penny, and nickel).

2. Explain that you are going to start off by making a prediction. Pretend to "work hard" thinking about your prediction. You might make it look like you're changing your mind as you think through it. Grab a small piece of paper and write on it, but don't let the spectator see that you are writing: "You will pick the quarter." Fold the piece of paper and put it into the cup. Speak aloud, "I just made a prediction. Now I'm going to fold up this paper, and put it into this cup for later."

3. Crayon: Spread the different crayons on the table. Tell the spectator to, "Pick any color crayon you want." Once they name a color, you pull that particular crayon or marker aside, and get rid of the rest.

4. Say, "Now I'm going to make a second prediction." Without the spectator seeing what you write, write down "You will pick the _____ [color] crayon." (The color of crayon you will write is the one that the spectator selected.) What's going on is the "one-ahead force." It is important that the spectator doesn't know that you're writing about the crayon now. The spectator will think that you are making a prediction about the next step, not the previous one.

5. Fingers: Ask the spectator to hold up any number of fingers between one and ten. Say aloud the number of fingers they held up. To give the spectator a feeling of freedom, you can say, "You could have held up any number of fingers, but you chose _____ [number]."

6. Say, "I'm going to make one final prediction." Write down the prediction secretly on another piece of paper, fold it, and put it into the cup. The prediction you will write will be "You will hold up _____ fingers."

7. Coins: Put the three different coins on the table: a quarter, penny, and nickel. Ask the spectator to point to any two of the coins. (Your goal is to secretly force them to pick the quarter—your first prediction.) So, here are the options:
- If the spectator happens to pick the nickel and the penny, say, "Okay, we'll get rid of these two, and we're left with the quarter."
- If they pick the quarter and penny, say, "Okay, we'll eliminate the dime." Then you ask them to push one of the two remaining coins toward you.
- If they push the penny toward you, say, "Okay, we'll eliminate the penny, and we're left with the quarter."
- If they push the quarter toward you, say, "Okay, you have selected the quarter."

No matter what happens, the spectator doesn't know that the rules of selection change depending on what coin you want to end up with.

8. Then you take the three predictions out of the cup and put them in the order you did the predictions (crayon color, number of fingers, and selected coin). One by one, you reveal that you correctly predicted each one.

Famous Foolers

Abracadabra!! Poof! No War

Magic can do more than entertain. In one true story, it actually stopped a rebellion. In the mid-1800s, France ruled Algeria, a colony in northern Africa. Algeria's leaders threatened to go to war with France. Some Algerian holy men were known for their "magical" skills, such walking on fire. So, the French decided to fight magic with magic. They contacted a French magician named Jean Eugène Robert-Houdin. The French leaders asked Robert-Houdin to create a magic trick that was so impressive the Algerian leaders would back down.

On October 28, 1856, a group of Algerian leaders were invited to a magic show by Robert-Houdin. After some dazzling tricks, Robert-Houdin brought out a wooden box with a metal handle and challenged a brawny Algerian leader to lift it. He did so. Then Robert-Houdin waved his hands, and said, "You are now weak." When the leader tried to pick up the box again, he couldn't! Next, Robert-Houdin invited a child to the stage, and the child lifted the box without a problem. By the end of the show, the Algerian leaders were so stunned, they stopped their revolt.

What was the secret to Robert-Houdin's trick? Underneath the stage was a powerful electromagnet. This type of magnet uses electricity and can be turned on and off. So, when Robert-Houdin pretended to cast his spell, an assistant flipped a switch that turned on the electromagnet. When the child was asked to lift the box, the electromagnet was flipped off.

Robert-Houdin believed the Algerian leaders should know the truth. So, he wrote them a letter explaining the secret. They were so impressed with his skill as an entertainer that they vowed to stay loyal to France.

Fool-ology

The Trickiest Audience Ever: Kids!

Some brain scientists were curious about which group of people were easier to fool: children or adults. So, they did an experiment. The scientists predicted that kids would be the ones who would be tricked easier. After all, they have less experience in life, so are more gullible, right? WRONG. Adult brains are very good at focusing on one thing at a time, quickly looking for patterns, and ignoring distractions. Kid brains, on the other hand, are easily distracted, have less experience with patterns, and have more curiosity.

Why does this matter in magic? Because magicians try to make the audience focus their attention one thing (the distraction), while they secretly do the tricky stuff elsewhere. Also, unlike adults, children know a lot less about how the world works, so they have fewer expectations and are less likely to find a quick pattern to explain something. Finally, children are more likely to ask questions at every second of a trick, whereas adults are more likely to jump ahead, overconfident that they think they know it all.

In the Blink of an Eye

To find out how magicians fool their crowd, some scientists have used special machines to observe eye movements of a magician's audience. They found that while watching a magic trick, the magician's pattern and movements cause the audience members to blink at key moments. Other brain research has shown that when we blink, our attention is lower than normal. By telling stories and causing the audience to laugh, the magician relaxes the audience, so they are not thinking as critically.

Con Artists, Mind Readers, and Other Scammers

Magicians are not the only people who love to fool us!

There are other professional tricksters who mess with our minds for fun and profit.

HEY, WHERE DID EVERYBODY GO?

Con Artists

Unlike painters and sculptors, these artists don't work with paint or marble. Their art usually involves wool...which they enjoy pulling over our eyes.

How Con Artists Dupe Us

People who rip off others by tricking them are known as *con artists*. The "con" stands for "confidence," and these rascals gain our confidence just long enough for us to give them our money. Unlike robbers, they don't break the law by stealing with a weapon or with threats. No, their method of robbing us is way sneakier.

According to neuroscientist Paul Zak, "The key to a con is not that you trust the con man, but that he shows he trusts you." When we help other people, our brains release the chemical *oxytocin*, which makes us feel good—so good that we feel the urge to trust the other person. We don't realize until it is too late that we've been had.

One of the most infamous "cons" is the Pigeon Drop Scam. To show you how it works, here are the renowned Royal Cranium Players to present a short play about it. *Presenting...Brian D. Brain, Mr. Shady, and Ms. Shifty.*

The Pigeon Drop Scam

Read this play out loud with some friends! Feel free to switch around the genders of the characters.

Setting: A public square, a lovely fall day

[Mr. Shady, a well-dressed fellow, is looking very confused.]

MR. SHADY: Excuse me! Could I talk to you for a minute?

BRIAN: Sure. What's up?

MR. SHADY: I'm lost, and I'm trying to get to an important job interview. Can you help me find Clark Street?

BRIAN: Sure, it's just a few blocks away. I'll give you directions.

[A few minutes later Ms. Shifty walks by Brian and Mr. Shady, and subtly drops a thick envelope near their feet.]

MS. SHIFTY: Pardon me, gentlemen. Did either of you drop this envelope?

MR. SHADY (as he picks it up): Not me. How about you?

BRIAN: No, I didn't.

MR. SHADY: Let's look inside it. Maybe it has some information so we can figure out who it belongs to.

[Mr. Shady opens it, and it is filled with LOTS of money.]

MR. SHADY: "Geez, there's like $500 in here! But there's no name. What should we do?

PSSST! AT NO TIME DURING THE PRESENTATION OF "THE PIGEON DROP" WILL ANY BIRDS BE DROPPED OR HARMED IN ANY WAY. IN FACT, THE WORD "PIGEON" IS AN OLD-TIMEY WORD MEANING SOMEONE WHO IS THE VICTIM OF A SCAM.

MS. SHIFTY: I think the three of us should split it. After all, we found it. And the money was probably stolen. You two in?

MR. SHADY: Sure. It's our lucky day.

BRIAN: (a little nervous) I guess so.

MR. SHADY: But before we get too greedy, I have an idea. Why don't you two wait here with the money, and I'll go in this store to see if anyone reported it lost?"

[Mr. Shady hands the envelope to Brian.]

MS. SHIFTY: Okay, that makes sense. (to Brian) You hold the envelope until he comes back.

BRIAN: Okay.

MR. SHADY: Wait, how do I know that I can trust you? What if I go into the store and you two split the dough and run off?

BRIAN: I won't do that.

MS. SHIFTY: Me, neither.

MR. SHADY: I guess, but just to play it safe, why don't each of you give me $50 right now? Just a sign that I can trust you not to run off with the envelope.

[Ms. Shifty gives Mr. Shady $50 from his wallet.]

MS. SHIFTY: That sounds fair. Here you go.

BRIAN (reluctantly): Well, okay. I guess so.

[Brian gives Mr. Shifty a 50 dollar bill.]

MS. SHIFTY: I promise, I'll be right back.

[A little while later...]

MS. SHIFTY: Hmm... I wonder what's keeping our new friend.

BRIAN: Maybe we should just go to the police!

MS. SHIFTY: Are you crazy? They'll think WE stole the money.

BRIAN: Maybe we should check on that guy in the store.

MS. SHIFTY: Yes, that's a smart idea. You hold the envelope of money, and I'll be back in a few minutes.

[Brian stands alone with the money. A few minutes later...]

BRIAN: I wonder where those guys went. Strange that they left me with all this money!

[Brian opens the envelope to see it is filled with scraps of worthless magazine clippings the size of paper money.]

BRIAN: What?! They switched the envelopes on me! This one's filled with old paper that's the same size as money. I've been SCAMMED!

[The End]

Creative Con Artists

Fooling Them on the Job

Ferdinand Waldo Demara Jr. (1921–1982), nicknamed "The Great Imposter," enjoyed doing things he wasn't trained to do. During the 1940s and 50s, he pretended to be a doctor, an engineer, a monk, a professor, a lawyer, and a teacher. During the Korean War in the 1950s, he worked on a Canadian battleship as a doctor—

even though he had never gone to medical school. Using his photographic memory and high intelligence, he studied medical textbooks in his room on the ship and learned how to do surgery. Demara once removed a bullet from a patient's chest. He saved many lives before he was caught.

Thinking Outside the Box

In the mid-1700s, Barbara Erni (1743–1785), an attractive daughter of homeless parents, traveled the country of Liechtenstein in Europe, dressed as a wealthy woman. Barbara traveled with a large trunk that she said was filled with treasures. At fancy inns or hotels, she'd tell the innkeepers, "I will be willing to stay here if—and only if—you make sure my trunk is safe. Would you promise to put it in the same room where you store your valuables?" Since she was elegantly dressed and acted rich, they believed her. The next morning, both Barbara and her trunk would be gone—along with other people's valuables that were in the room with the trunk. It turns out Barbara had an accomplice (secret partner): a very small man who hid in the trunk. At night, this man would sneak out of the trunk, steal all

the valuables in the room, and then escape. No one knows what happened to Erni's accomplice, but she was caught, confessed to the robberies, and was beheaded.

The Money Making Machine

Victor Lustig (1890–1947) knew where to find wealthy suckers—cruise ships. In the 1920s, he sailed on fancy ships between Paris and New York, telling people he was a royal count. He was well dressed and spoke many languages.

One of his most famous cons was his money machine. He showed passengers how it worked: He put a real $100 bill inside it, and then waited six hours for "chemical processing." Afterward, he'd remove two real $100 bills from the machine. Then another six hours later, it would produce another real $100 bill. Passengers were amazed, and greedy. Lustig would tell them the money box wasn't for sale, but the more he protested, the more they wanted one. Eventually, Lustig would secretly sell it for as much as $40,000. The people who bought Lustig's machine were thrilled when it made $100 bills every six hours. But after the first few $100 bills came out, the machines only printed blank paper! By the time they realized they were scammed, Lustig was long gone.

He "Made Off" with a Fortune

Thousands of people trusted Bernie Madoff with their money. He promised that if they gave him their hard-earned cash, his company would invest it in stocks and make them wealthy. Madoff was a respected stockbroker with many famous clients. Not only that, many of Madoff's family members invested with him, and he supported many worthwhile charities.

The problem with Madoff's investment plan was that it was based on something called a *Ponzi* scheme (named after Charles Ponzi, another sneaky criminal). In this scam, the con artist uses money from new investors to pay back the older investors. This type of investment plan works for a while but eventually collapses. Once the number of investors grows and grows, any risky investments might cause everyone involved to lose piles of money. On top of that, Madoff kept most of the money for himself. By the time he was caught, he had tricked his investors out of $65 billion. Many people lost their life savings. Madoff was caught in 2009, pled guilty, and was sentenced to 150 years in jail.

Marks

Con artists are experts in human psychology. Their first step is finding the perfect "mark" or victim. Retired FBI agent Mike Connelley said, "Many marks are people who believe they are getting something for nothing." Con artists sniff out people who are desperate, lonely, or greedy. They figure out what the mark really wants and then how they can help the person think they'll get it. Knowing this information is very important if the con artist is going to show empathy and bond with their victim.

Can Some People REALLY Read Minds?

Psychics claim they have the power to delve into our innermost thoughts and predict the future. It doesn't matter whether they use crystal balls or tarot cards, or do palm readings. As soon as we part with our money, they share remarkable details about our family, friends, health, school, jobs, and more. We think, "How true! How amazing!" But it's all an act by a clever charlatan (a fancy word for trickster). What's really going on?

The Art of Cold Reading

When a psychic meets a new customer, they do a cold reading. This technique uses some sneaky mind tricks to make the person believe she knows a lot about them, even though they have never met. Here are some of the most popular:

Setting the Scene

Before doing the reading, a psychic will set the expectations by saying that she's not perfect, but if the customer cooperates, she'll try her best. The reading is set up as a team effort. This puts gentle pressure on the customer if things aren't working out. If the psychic makes a wrong guess, she might say, "Look into my eyes and let's try harder."

Shotgunning

When addressing a large group of people, a psychic will offer some very general statements that probably fit for someone, such as "I see someone with an elderly relative who is ill," and "Someone here once had a very difficult time in their math class." The psychic pays careful attention to body language to tell if she is on the right track. Is the person smiling or fidgeting?

Fishing

A psychic throws out a number of very specific guesses in the same sentence, hoping that at least one will match. "I'm sensing that someone in your family has a name that starts with an A, an M, or maybe a J?" Again, many people will respond with, "Yes, my older sister's name is Miranda," for instance. An another time a psychic might say, "I sense there's a 2 or 5 or 7 in your phone number." And this gives the psychic more information.

Hot Topics

Most people go to a fortune teller for the same reasons. They want to find out about love, work, health, money, school, and travel. By sticking to these themes, the customer is more open to sharing information. They might say, "You want someone to become a new friend, but you're worried they might not like you as much as you like them. Does this sound right?"

Barnum Statements

This type of statement, named after P.T. Barnum, the American circus creator, sounds personal but is actually true about most people. The psychic might say, "You are usually positive and upbeat, but there's a time not too long ago, when you were upset." Or maybe she'll say, "When you are in a new situation, you tend to feel shy and somewhat insecure." Duh!

Rainbow Ruse

This sort of statement says two opposite observations, so it can never be wrong. The psychic might say, "You are usually kind and thoughtful, but when someone acts selfishly, you can get angry."

BRIAN: I can see into your future. You will meet a young girl as beautiful as a princess.

FROG: Yes, yes, tell me more!

BRIAN: She will be very curious and want to know everything about you!

FROG: Will I meet her in a castle?

BRIAN: No, a biology class!

You have a strong desire to be liked by others, but there are times when you prefer to be alone. At times, you are extroverted and sociable, at other times you are shy and reserved.

Magician Debunks Mediums

Famous magician and escape artist Harry Houdini spent much of his career debunking mediums, who claimed to communicate with dead spirits. As a master of fooling people for entertainment, Houdini was convinced these mediums were fakes, taking advantage of others for money. In the 1920s, a woman named Mina "Margery" Crandon said she could use her powers to talk with her dead brother, Walter. At special events called séances, Margery would turn off the lights, and conjure up Walter's gruff voice, or have his "spirit" tip over tables, ring bells, or play trumpets. She would also have a gooey slime called "ectoplasm" ooze out her nose and ears. Houdini was determined to put her "powers" to the test. During the séance, Houdini noticed her secretly moving the table and objects. He wrote a pamphlet showing how she did each of her psychic tricks. Houdini explained that Margery was talented at using her feet under the table to ring a bell during the séance. The "ectoplasm" was later found to be bits of cloth or even a sheep's lung.

Horoscopes

Do you believe that horoscopes really predict your future? Many people do. They look at the horoscope page in the newspaper because they believe their astrological sign tells them about their future. What horoscope fans don't realize is that all the horoscope descriptions are made of Barnum Statements (see page 68). In other words, they apply to everyone, but they seem specific.

Experiments

Pull out the horoscope page of a local newspaper and ask a friend or family member to tell you his or her birthday, so you can figure out his or her sign. In other words, are they an Aquarius, Sagittarius, and so on? Then tell each person you'll read her horoscope, and afterward ask how accurate it is on a scale of 1 to 5. The secret is that you deliberately read the wrong horoscope for each person and see what the person says. Repeat this experiment with 5 to 10 people. What did most people say? Afterwards, reveal the truth and tell them you were doing a science experiment. As an alternative, you can ask a group of ten people to tell you their astrological sign, and then you reach into a folder and hand each person a folded piece of paper with their "personal horoscope" on it. (All the papers are actually identical, but don't reveal this yet.) Ask: How accurate is it? Once each person has read their paper, have them trade papers with another person. They'll discover they are all the same!

Professional Foolers

Do you have a talent for tricking others? If so, perhaps your future career could be one of the following. Each of the following jobs involves deceiving others.

Undercover Police Officer

To catch criminals, some police officers have to go "undercover" as the bad guys. To be believable, they act as "un-cop-like" as possible, so they can become friends with the criminals they want to catch. They have to dress and talk like those that want to break the law. By getting close to the criminals, officers bring criminals to justice. Being an undercover officer can be thrilling and interesting but also stressful and extremely dangerous.

Undercover Journalists

This profession combines writing skill with detecting ability. They dig up the truth about organizations that do not want to share its secrets with the world. So, in order to write the detailed truth, the journalist has to lie about why he or she is there. In the 1880s, a daring reporter named Elizabeth Jane Cochrane, who wrote under the name Nellie Bly, wanted to find out why patients were treated so horribly in a famous "insane asylum" in New York City.

So, she acted crazy enough to get herself admitted as a patient. She dressed herself in tattered clothes, didn't bathe or brush her teeth, and always had a strange smile. Once inside, she wrote reports that were published in the newspaper. She reported about how terribly the patients were treated and how unclean the asylum was. The public was outraged. Her writing pressured the government to give more money and attention to the asylum and to give the patients better care.

Athletes

Some sports require their players to be tricky to succeed. Basketball players, for example, are famous for dribbling the ball down the court, then appearing to pass it to the right—but instead holding the ball for a moment and quickly passing it to the left. Hockey and soccer players also use fake-out techniques to fool the goalies, so they won't know what side the puck or ball will be aimed at, or when the shot will be taken. Even when athletes know that fake-outs are possible, they usually can't react fast enough to before the point is made.

Advertisers

The main goal of advertisers is to make you buy particular products. Getting people to part with their cash can be challenging, but they are more likely to do so if the products look perfect.

Food Ads

Breakfast cereal gets soggy in milk so when creating pictures for magazines, advertisers use white glue, which keeps the cereal looking crisp. A photo of delicious-looking BBQ chicken might actually look amazing because the chicken has small amounts of black shoe polish on it. Ads of glistening fruits and veggies look super fresh until you learn that they often use hair spray to make them sparkle.

A Brainy Business

Even the lettering on packaging can be tricky. Since we feel more connected to products that remind us of happy people, advertisers might tilt up the lower case "e's" in words to make them look like smiles. Advertisers also use psychology to make us want to buy something. One technique is to say, "Buy now before they're gone!" We can feel a sense of panic about missing out.

Another trick advertisers use to hook our attention is to use the brain psychology of "mirror neurons." They create images that quickly persuade our emotions by making neurons in our brain connect with the pictures and sounds in the ad. If we see a person in a commercial thrilled about a particular product, our brains are made to want to imitate that experience. It's like when you see someone yawn, you feel like yawning, too.

Foolproof Your Brain

By now, you know that our brains can't be trusted all the time.

Our senses sometimes misinterpret the outside world, we are easily distracted, our memories are often sketchy, and our emotions can interfere with our thinking.

The good news is your days of being easily fooled are over. Step right up and read the incredible scientific research in this chapter. You'll be shocked at how your intelligence will reach amazing new heights and you will never again be tricked by crooked people who want to swindle your money.

WHAT'RE WE TALKING ABOUT? OH, ZEBRAS, THAT'S RIGHT . . . WAIT, THAT'S NOT IT.

Did you buy that baloney? Sure, it would be really nice to never be deceived but sadly that's not possible. Everyone—even the smartest people in the world—can be fooled in some situations. In fact, the very people who insist that they can never be tricked are often the most easily deceived. Their arrogance gets in the way of thinking clearly. Nobel Prize–winning physicist Richard Feynman said, "The first principle is that you must not fool yourself, and you are the easiest person to fool." But if you read this chapter carefully and do the activities, you will be less likely to be fooled.

> "I used to think that the brain was the most wonderful organ in my body. Then I realized who was telling me this." — *COMEDIAN EMO PHILIPS*

The Truth About Lying

Even the most honest people lie. It's nearly impossible to tell the truth 24/7. This is especially true when you are trying to spare someone's feelings. For instance, it looks like a squirrel cut your friend's hair with a weed whacker. He asks if you like it. Hmm... Another common situation is lying when you make a mistake because you don't want to get caught. "No, it was broken when I got here." If the lie works, there are no consequences.

Professor Dan Ariely from Duke University was curious how greed would make people lie. He set up an experiment in which each participant had to answer twenty math problems. The problems weren't hard, but he only gave them five minutes to complete them. They were told they would get $1 for every question they answered correctly. No one was able to finish all the questions. Afterward, each participant was asked to take their test paper to the front of the room and put it in a paper shredder. Next, the experimenter looked them in the eye and asked them how many questions they got right, and paid them accordingly. What the participants didn't know was that the shredder was fixed. It only shredded the sides, so the scientists could see who was telling the truth.

They found that, on average, most people solved only four problems correctly—but told the researchers they got six right. Ariely's team concluded that "Lots of people cheat a little bit; very, very few people cheat a lot." In a twist on this experiment, they gave people plastic tokens for every correct answer, and the people then had to walk to the other side of the room and turn in these tokens for money. Ariely discovered that this change made people lie twice as much! He concluded that the tokens were one step removed from the cash, so people felt more comfortable cheating the scientists.

Spotting a Liar

Security officers at the airport are constantly trying to find liars. This sort of detective work is very tricky. After much research, experts have discovered some clues for telling if someone is lying.

Eye contact doesn't matter.
Some people believe that people avoid eye contact when they tell a lie. Not so! People who tell lies actually make more eye contact than normal as if to say, "How could I be lying, dude? I'm staring right at you!"

Observe body language.
Lying is hard work for our brains. If we feel guilty about lying, it can pop out in how we move our body. Maybe we fidget more, clear our throat a lot, or move our heads slightly backwards. Psychologist Nancy Etcoff found that people who have a language-processing disorder were much better at spotting liars than those without the disorder. This is probably because they were not distracted by the liar's words.

Ask open questions.
This is so the liar can get caught in their explanation. Better to ask, "Why do you think there are only two cookies left in the jar?" than, "Did you take the cookies from the jar?"

Dig for specific details.
By asking for specific information that you can check, this can break down a liar's confidence.

Use the element of surprise.
Put the liar's brain to work by asking them to explain the details out of order, such as backwards in time.

Listen to "honesty language."
If someone says, "To be perfectly honest with you" or "to tell the truth," they might be bending over backward to "prove" they aren't being dishonest.

Keep it casual.
The more someone feels they are being interrogated, the less likely they are to accidentally spill the beans by telling facts that don't line up.

Wink! You're DEAD!

In this classic game, you commit murders by winking your eye. But will you get caught?

What You Need

At least 6 friends (the more the better)

What to Do

1. Everyone but one person stands in a circle and closes his or her eyes. That one person has a special role.

2. The person not in the round walks around the outside of the circle a few times and taps one person once on the shoulder to indicate that person is the murderer. The person on the outside of the circle taps a second person twice to indicate that person is the detective.

3. All players open their eyes. The person outside the circle sits off to the side. The detective moves to the center of the circle and tries to figure out who the murderer is by asking the players questions. They might ask, "Are you the murderer?" "Would you lie to me?" They can be tricky by asking each person something they know is a lie, "Do you like to dance?" "Are you fond of eating peas?"

4. While this is going on, the person picked as the Murderer "kills" other players by winking at them. If a player is winked at, her or she has to dramatically die and leave the circle. The detective has three chances to guess the murderer. If they can't, they have to stay as detective the next round.

Build Your Own Baloney Detector

Don't you wish there were a special, portable gizmo you could wear that would secretly tell you when someone is trying to pull a fast one on you? Like your own personal lie detector? If you had such a device, you could tell when someone is trying to sell you something expensive that is actually worthless. You'd know when a friend, family member, or politician was lying to you. And you'd know if some outrageous claim was the truth or just a hoax.

The good news is that your brain has the power to do this job. Scientists call this ability "being skeptical" and "using critical thinking." By developing certain thinking skills, you give your brain a better Baloney Detector. (The famous scientist Carl Sagan coined this funny term.) If you follow these guidelines, you are much less likely to be fooled.

1. ASK LOTS OF QUESTIONS.

What reasons do I have to think this might be true?

What reasons do I have to think it might be false?

Is it April Fool's Day? If so, chances are the wild claim is a prank!

Is it too good to be true? If so, then it is probably not based in fact.

Does your "gut" tell you something is off? (Trust your gut. The moment you suspect something is a scam, walk away or hang up the phone. Don't get hooked.)

2. ANALYZE THE FACTS.

What do other people say? Ask other people who can help you find facts to back up this idea, such as librarians, teachers, scientists, and so on.

Check all the facts in a few different places. Don't be swayed by, "It must be true, I read it on the Internet!" Just because something is in print or on a screen, doesn't make it true.

Who is the "authority" backing a claim? Will they make money or gain something else if you believe them?

What are alternate explanations? If you think "A" happened because of "B," is it possible that "B" actually caused "A?" Or maybe something else entirely caused "A"?

3. ANALYZE YOUR LOGIC.

It's easy to confuse coincidence with causation. That's a fancy way of saying that just because two things happen at the same time doesn't mean that one necessarily caused the other. For example, you wore green socks when you took your big math test, and then you aced it. So, the green socks obviously caused your success, right? Or was it a coincidence?

Kid: "Um, Brian, what's with the parrot on your head?"

Brian: "Oh, that! I wear it to keep the elephants away!"

Kid: "But there are no elephants around here!"

Brian: "See? It's working!"

4. CHECK IN WITH YOUR EMOTIONS AND BELIEFS.

Are your feelings getting in the way of your thinking? Just because you really, really want something to be true doesn't make it so. Does it sound too good to be true?

Humans like to think they're right. So, if we hear a new idea or fact that goes against what we already think, our natural urge is to reject it or be very suspicious. To have a strong Baloney Detector, resist loving your ideas so much that you ignore evidence that doesn't support them.

5. CAN IT BE TESTED?

Any wild idea that can't be tested in an experiment can't be proven true—or false. Also, don't fall into the mistake that just because something is a mystery today doesn't mean that it can never be explained.

6. SAYS WHO?

If you're consulting "experts" to check the facts or back up a claim, what is their background? Beware of statements beginning with vague phrases, such as "Studies show..." and "Experts say..." They could be totally made up or based on really poor studies.

7. DON'T JUMP TO CONCLUSIONS.

Just because a wild idea can't be explained doesn't mean that it is forever a mystery, and we'll never know. We might not have the tools to answer the question right now.

Don't complain when your brain
Acts dumb or insane
Or gets snookered and suckered and fooled.
That pink, squishy blob
Is just doing its job.
So what if you sometimes get schooled?

It jumps to conclusions,
Gets tricked by illusions,
And lets con artists and others deceive you.
Its rational notions
Are swayed by emotions.
It makes clever thoughts up and leaves you.

To err is human that goes twice for your mind,
But I think you will find
It is wrongly maligned!

Every second your noggin is sloggin' away,
It's trying its best just to get through the day.
Its billions of neurons are hit with sensations,
And trillions of choices and mental frustrations
And misinformation and exaggerations
No wonder your brain takes lots of vacations!

So, don't complain
when your brain
Is a runaway train
With its shortcuts and
glitches and flaws.
It's neurotic and nutty
And acts silly as putty.
It deserves our respect
just because.
Yeah, it's shady and shoddy
But it still runs your body.
So, give it a round of applause!

Glossary

Amygdala: Part of the limbic system of the brain that control emotions, especially fear

Barnum statements: Named after the famous circus creator, these are statements that sound personal but are actually true about most people. Used by psychics.

Brain hemispheres: The cerebrum of the brain is divided into two halves called hemispheres that are connected by a bridge of nerves.

Brain stem: Located at the base of the brain, it controls breathing, heartbeat, food digestion, and body temperature.

Cerebellum: Located below the cerebrum of the brain, it controls bodily movements.

Cerebral cortex: The outer layer of the cerebrum of the brain

Cerebrum: The largest part of the brain, which controls conscious and voluntary processes.

Cold read: A series of tricks psychics use to pretend they know a lot about someone they just met.

Doppler effect: A change in the frequency of a wave as the observer and source move toward or away from each other.

Frequency: How quickly sound waves travel through the air

Frontal lobe: Part of the cerebrum that controls thinking, talking, planning, organizing, solving problems, and paying attention

Hippocampus: This section of the limbic system collects information from the working memory of the cerebrum and stores it as memories.

Hypothalamus: This section of the limbic system collects information about body temperature, sleepiness, hunger, and thirst.

Limbic system: Part of the brain that controls feelings, memories, and learning. Nicknamed "the lizard brain."

Misdirection: The action of directing someone's attention to the wrong place

Neurons: Nerve cells that use chemicals and electricity to send signals to and from the brain

Notes: The group of pitches, in order, that makes musical scales

Occipital Lobe: Part of the cerebrum that controls information about vision.

Octave: A series of eight notes, when two notes have a similar sound but one is higher or lower than the original note

Parietal lobe: Part of the cerebrum that monitors and controls body movement, reading, sense of touch, and more

Peripheral vision: Side vision; what is seen on either side when the eyes are looking straight ahead

Photoreceptor cells: Cells found in the retina of the eye that convert light into signals that are sent to the brain

Pitch: The sound produced, based on its frequency

Ponzi scheme: A fraud in which money is paid to early investors with the money invested by people who have invested later

Saccades: Rapid, jumpy eye movements from one eye position to another

Smooth pursuit: When your eyes move smoothly instead of in jumps

Temporal lobe: Part of the cerebrum that interprets sounds, language, and recognizes objects, and it's where memories are made

Thalamus: Part of the limbic system of the brain responsible for sight, sound, taste, and touch

Answers for page 31

1) "Imagination is more important than knowledge."—Albert Einstein; 2) You must do the things you think you cannot do.—Eleanor Roosevelt; 3) "I spent most of my time in school daydreaming and managed to turn it into a living."—George Lucas; 4) I used to think the brain was the most wonderful organ in my body. Then I realized who was telling me this!"—Emo Philips; 5) The human brain has 100 billion neurons, each neuron connected to 10 thousand other neurons. Sitting on your shoulders is the most complicated object in the known universe.—Michio Kaku

Index